Tattooing is alive and well. In fact it is thriving like never before. *Our Tattoos* 'best of' book strives to bring the most exciting and talented artists to you, but in all honesty we have barely even began to scratch the surface.

This unprecedented tattoo craze has spread to all the corners of the globe and due to far more free communication between artists and the sharing of knowledge it has been lifted to amazing new heights. It is our hope that this publication can help encourage this positive growth and showcase this movement.

More than ever the customer expects and deserves his or her tattoo to be done by someone with passion, skill and with respect to the whole process.

Tattooing is permanent but only in the sense that the client wears the tattoo for the remainder of their life, but who knows if this tattoo is looked after properly in the healing process and even makes it that long. As a tattooer we put years of practice, refining our craft leading up to the moment of the tattoo. To then have, in most cases, never a chance to see the end result again after it's completed. So permanence is really a matter of perspective. A single photo is sometimes the only reminder. Often this is not possible as the light can be wrong or the tattoo wraps the body or the client is in too much pain to clean it properly for a nice photo, or simply your camera is flat.

Even when photos are taken they can never truly do justice to a tattoo and show the harmony of a well-applied tattoo to the skin and the reflection of the person's own feelings and personality with in it. But it is somewhat of a glimpse of this and we are here to show you a collection of these moments.

Within this book we have found a fresh and relevant group of today's best and hardworking tattooers to print. It is our hope to use *Our Tattoos* to preserve and share what we truly love about tattooing. Thanks for coming on this journey and for the continued support.

Looking to the future and respecting the past.

Bugsy & Adam

Vol. 1 Cover by Bugsy

Vol. 2 Cover by William Yoneyama

Vol. 3 Cover by Crispy Lennox

J.Ingemar 14

Vol. 4 Cover by Johann Ingemar

Vol. 5 Cover by Daniel Octoriver

How did each of you come to tattoo art?

Bugsy - I've been tattooing for 13 years. Getting my first tattoo was it. I knew I had to do tattoos, not just get them.

Adam - I was always upset when the temporary tattoos washed off so I decided to get real ones. Bugsy and I became friends after he drew on me with his pain pen

What do you aim to do with Our Tattoos?

B - Just to help promote tattooing in a positive way and focus on the tattooers that are really pushing the envelope. It is chance for me personally to give back to tattooing that has given me so much

A - For me it's about creating a quality product to showcase the amazing talents of tattoo artists. Our Tattoos is all about great tattoos. That is what we try to show with each issue just great tattoos. No ads, no bullshit, just straight up great tattoos. I want Our Tattoos to be something that I'm proud of and that tattoo artists are proud to be in

How is Our Tattoos changing from first editions?

B - The biggest change is the size. More pages is more artists, but this is great as it means we can focus on not only big names but up and comers. It also gives us a bit of room to make a nice spread on each artist, especially the ones that take a nice picture.

A - More artists, more pages and more tattoos. I think every issue is getting better.

What trends do you see in tattoo art?

B - The trend is that there is no trend. So many people with different tastes mean that there is a client out there for every good tattooer and vice versa. Little tricks and such pop up every now and then but it's an exciting thing to be involved in.

A - Its popularity. Tattoos are certainly becoming a lot more socially acceptable and as a consequence tattooing in general is gaining the respect it deserves as an art form. These can only mean good things for the tattoo industry.

Past trends-history?

B - People want originality, something personal and larger pieces. You can't sum yourself up in a 50 cent piece sized tattoo! Or its very sad if you could!!

A - In terms of tattoo styles I guess there have been periods where one style is more popular than another but I think that overall people just get tattoos of stuff they like.

Do you see and Future trends - temporary tattoos, different methods?

B - Who knows where it will go. I hope, despite the world moving faster and things becoming disposable, that tattooing can be a link back to something more primal.

A - In the future you will be able to buy a robot that will tattoo you with special nano particles that can change designs.

Who inspires you, tattoo greats, influences?

B - Tattooers are my heroes and my biggest influence. I admire many other people and artists etc. But at the end of the day tattooing is my life. Our Tattoos is an extension of that.

A - There is so many people out there doing amazing things that I am constantly inspired to create the best work I can whatever that is.

Comments, feedback from readers-fans? Critics?

B - I'm very influenced by good quality printed books we hope to make a magazine that is essentially as good as a book. The feedback has only been positive and from all over the world from the tattooers in it and from the customer.

A - I've only ever received positive feedback for Our Tattoos. The best feedback for me is from tattooists. I'm so grateful for every tattooist that trusts us with his or her images and it makes me very happy when tattooists appreciate what we do.

How do you actually go about putting an edition together, as compared to first editions?

B - The process is just getting faster and more regular. I pick someone I can work closely with to paint a cover and then build up a list of the best tattooers I can find that compliment each other and show the range of modern tattooing. I travel a lot and if I meet a good tattooer I ask them to be in it!!!

A- After receiving the images from the artists I go about putting it all together. For each artists I look at the number and quality of images I have to work with. From that I work out the page allocation. I then design each set of pages for each artists based on their images.

Do you see printed editions as worthwhile?

A - Even though there is a massive amount of digital content out there I think there is nothing like a printed mag you can hold in your hand and flick through the pages. And besides who wants to take their iPad into the shitter.

Other passions?

B - Tattooing is all consuming in my life. My friendships, including Adam, have all been made through tattooing and the bonds that have been created I cherish. Of course my family, friends and girlfriend are a huge part of my life but they all have to put up with tattooing and the love I have for it.

A - Family and friends. I also don't mind taking photos and are quite fond of science.

DONE WITH
ELECTRICITY

Published by:
Wilkinson Publishing Pty Ltd
ACN 006 042 173
Level 4, 2 Collins Street
Melbourne, Vic 3000
Tel: 03 9654 5446
www.wilkinsonpublishing.com.au

International distribution by Pineapple Media Limited
www.pineapple-media.com
ISSN 1838-6520

National Library of Australia Cataloguing-in-Publication entry

Author:	Lockman, Adam, author.
Other Authors/Contributors:	Christensen, Ian, author.
Title:	Our Tattoos : The best tattoos from the world's best artists. Vol. 4 Adam Lockman and Ian Christensen.
ISBN:	9781922178503 (paperback)
Subjects:	Body art. Tattoo artists. Tattooing--Pictorial works.
Dewey Number:	391.65

Adam Craft
Adam Kitamoto
Amanda Grace Leadman
Andrew McLeod
Austin Maples
Bailey Hunter Robinson
Brendan O'Connor
Brent Ryan
Capilli Tupou
Chad Koeplinger
Charley Gerardin
Christopher Marchetto
Clifton Carter
Crispy Lennox
Dan Aranda
Daniel Octoriver
Dave Bryant
Derrik Montez
Dusty Neal
Fergus Simms
Feroze McLeod
Gong
Gore
Hamish McLauchlan
Harry Morgan
Heath Crowe
Heath Nock
Holly Ellis
Jacob Des
James McKenna
Jasmin Austin
Jason Donahue
Javier Betancourt
Jelle Soos
Jenna Slowerblack
Jim Little
Joel Melrose
Johann Ingemar
Josh Leahy
Justin Burnout

Karl Willmann
Kid Kross
Kirk Jones
Lauren Winzer
Liam Jenkins
Liam Sparkes
Malika Rose
Mark Cross
Marshall
Matt Deverson
Matt Shamah
Matt Wisdom
Max May
Maxime Büchi
Meighan Mary
Mick Gore
Mitch 13
Mitch Love
Nick Rutherford
Noah Moore
Oliver Christenson
Pari Corbitt
Rempe
Rich Hardy
Rose Hardy
Ryan Shaffer
Sal Scutio
Sam Arrowsmith
Sam Kane
Sam Rulz
Sandi Calistro
Shane Gallagher
Simon Earl
Stacey Anne
Steve Byrne
Stevie Edge
Terry James
Wan
William Yoneyama
Zoe Dennis

Adam Craft

Vol. 2

Adam Kitamoto

Vol. 4

Amanda Grace Leadman

Vol. 2

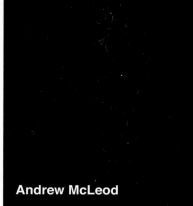

Andrew McLeod

Vol. 3

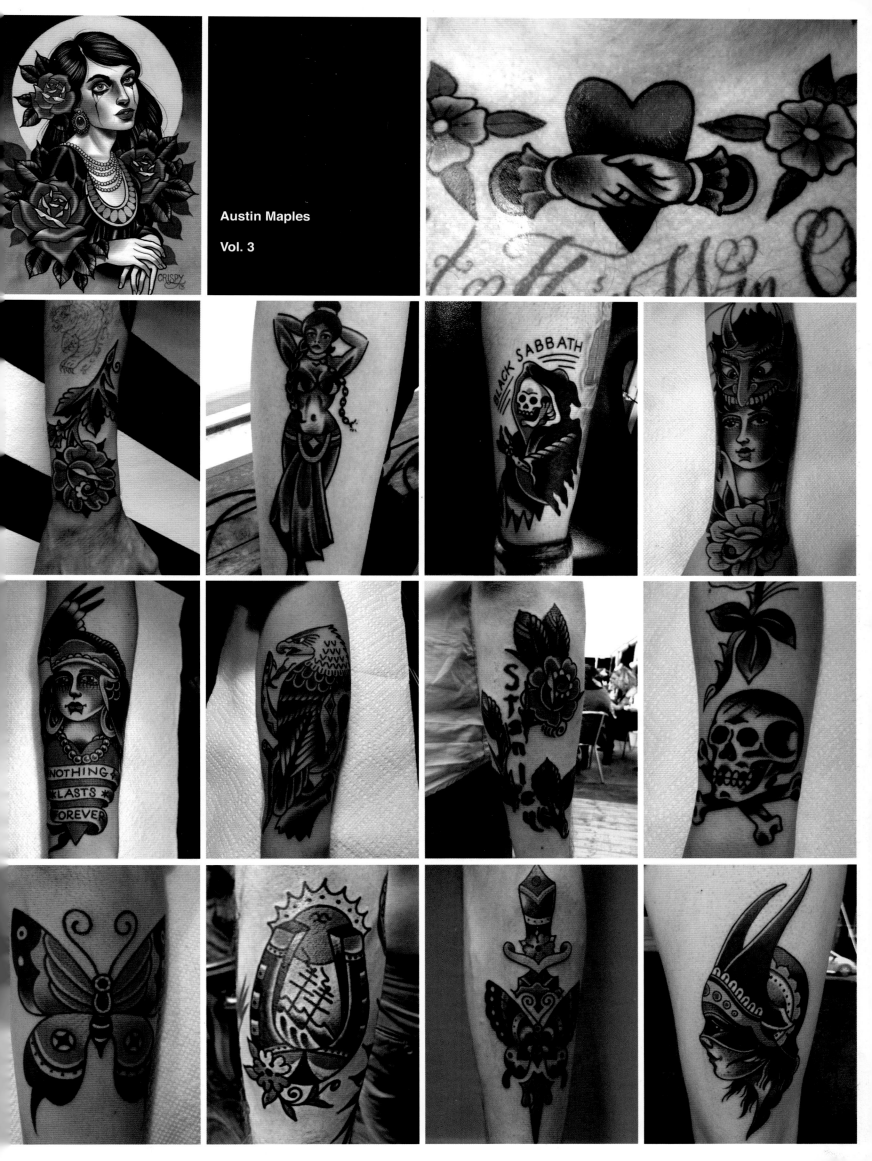

Austin Maples

Vol. 3

Bailey Hunter Robinson

Vol. 5

Brendan O'Connor

Vol. 5

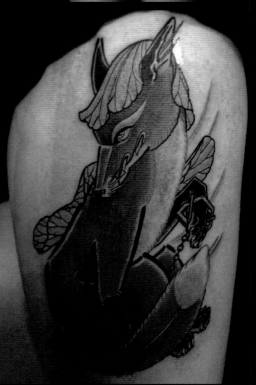

Brent Ryan

Vol. 1

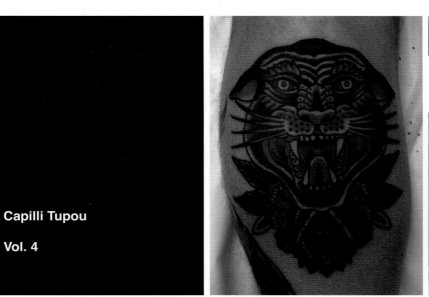

Capilli Tupou

Vol. 4

Chad Koeplinger

Vol. 1

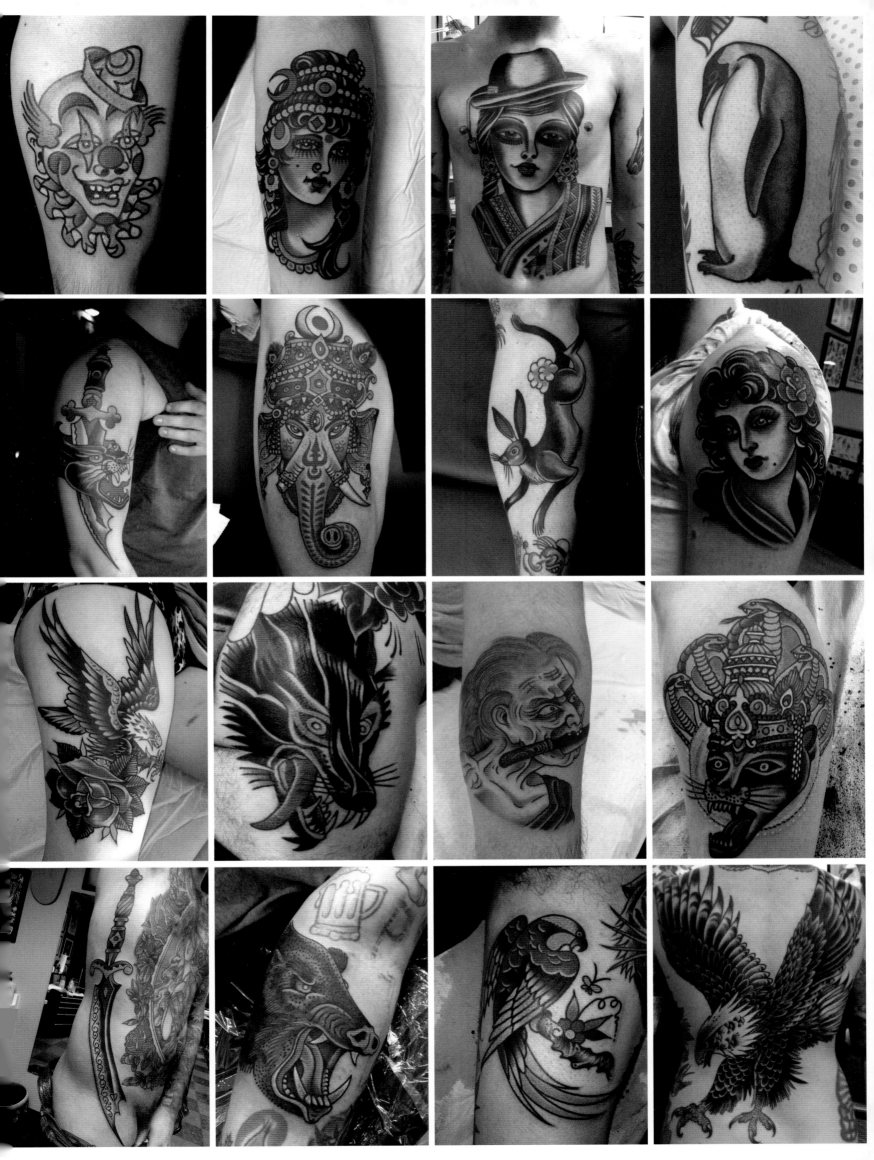

Charley Gerardin

Vol. 3

   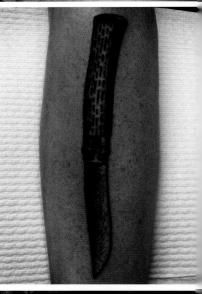

   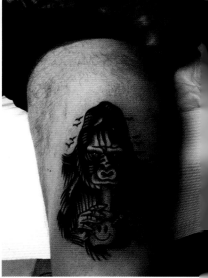

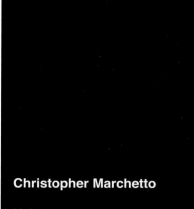

Christopher Marchetto

Vol. 4

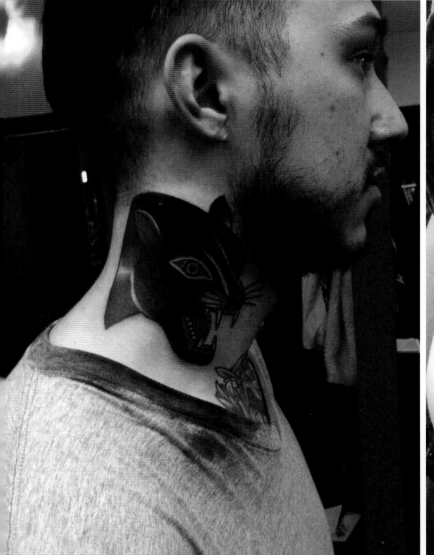

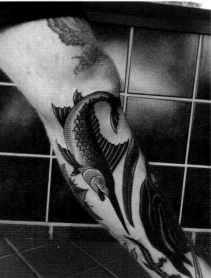

Clifton Carter

Vol. 3

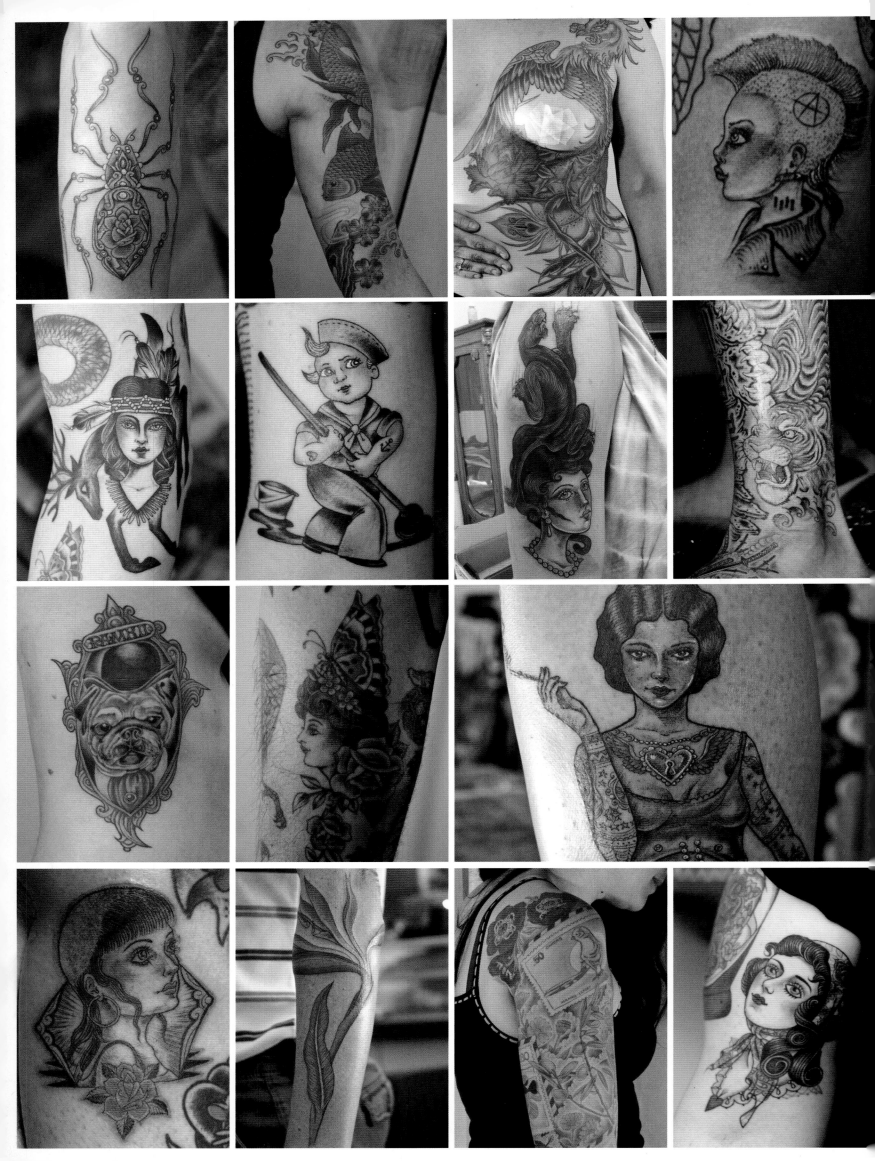

Crispy Lennox

Vol. 3

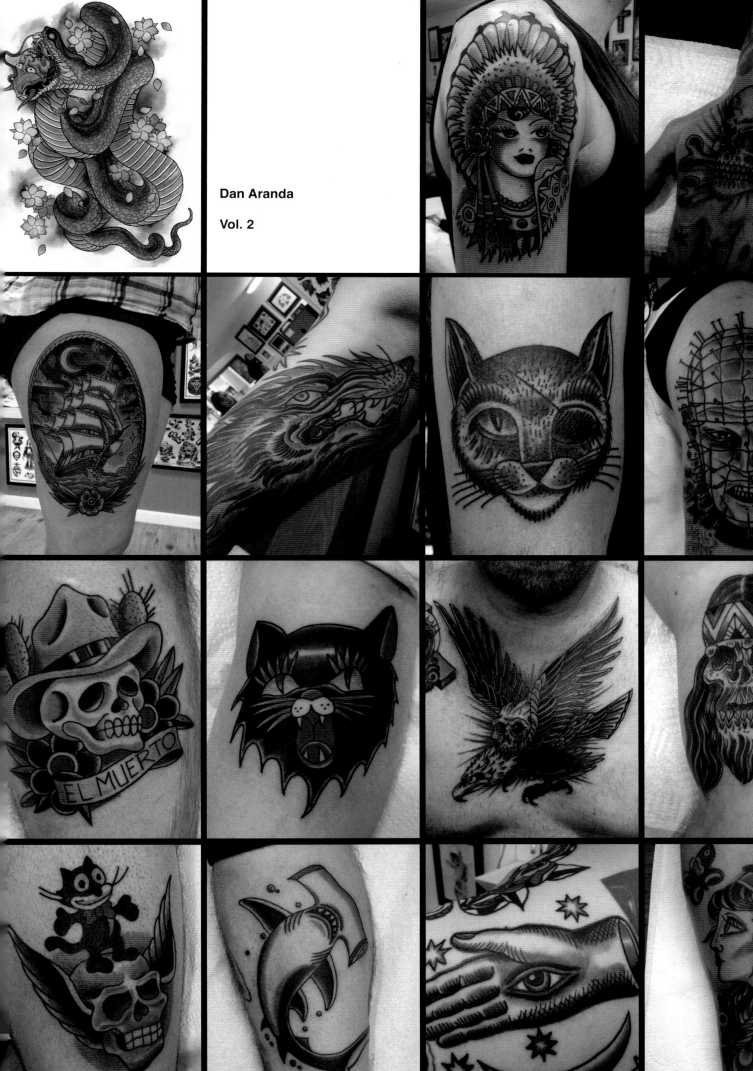

Dan Aranda

Vol. 2

Daniel Octoriver

Vol. 5

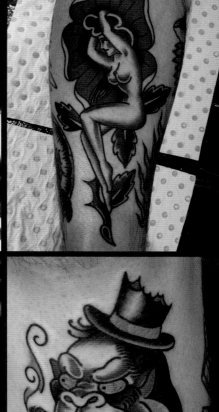

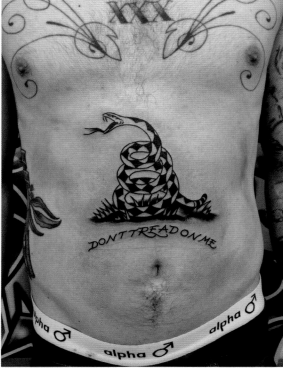

Dave Bryant

Vol. 1

Derrik Montez

Vol. 5

Dusty Neal

Vol. 4

Fergus Simms

Vol. 5

Feroze McLeod

Vol. 5

Gong

Vol. 5

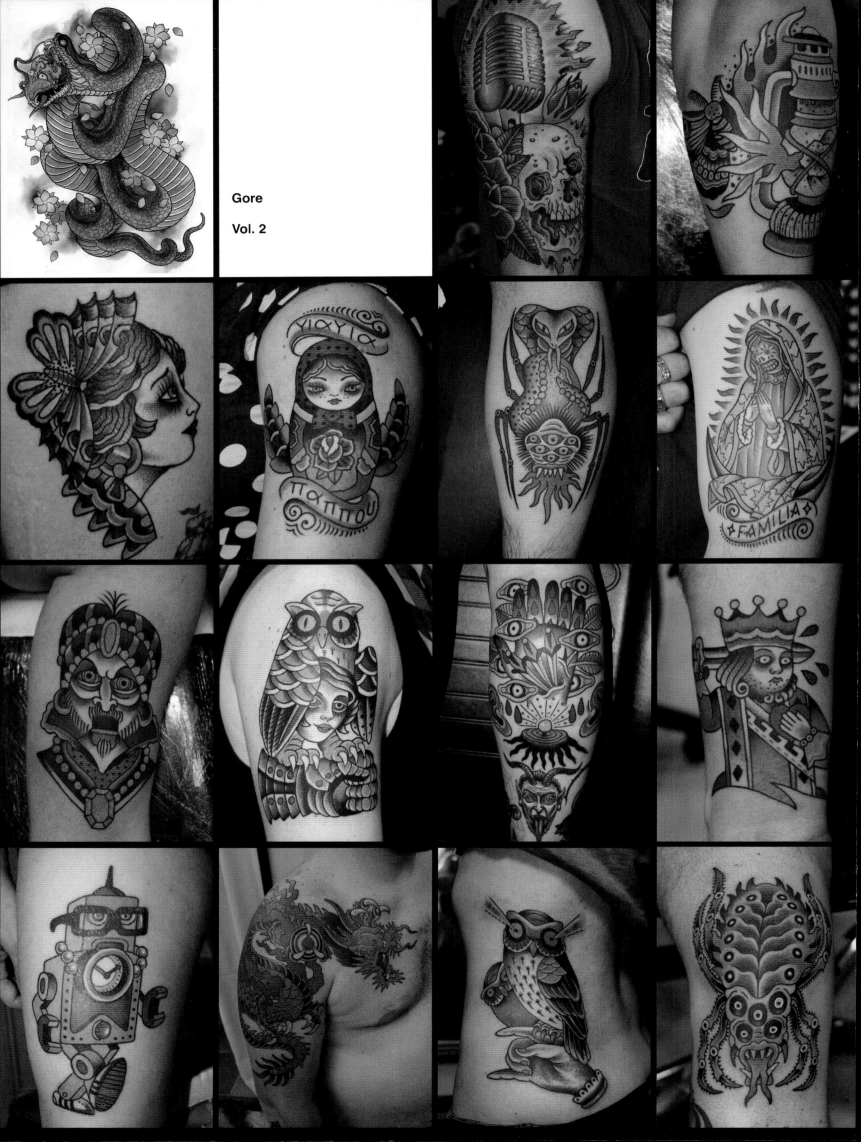

Gore

Vol. 2

Hamish McLauchlan

Vol. 5

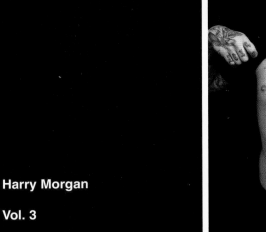

Harry Morgan

Vol. 3

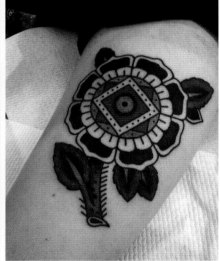

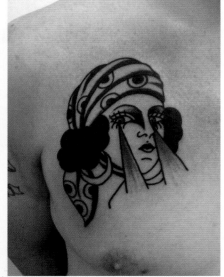

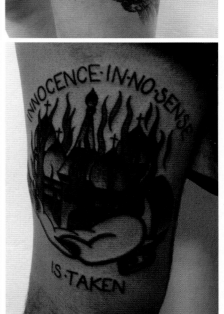

Heath Crowe

Vol. 2

Heath Nock

Vol. 2

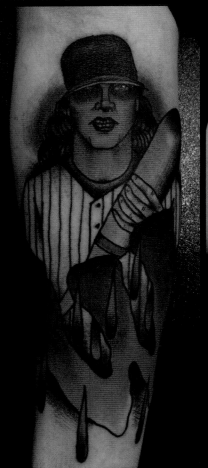

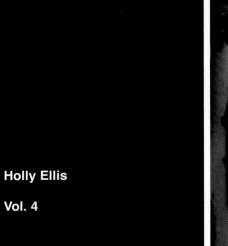

Holly Ellis

Vol. 4

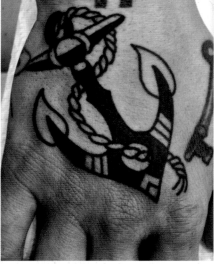

Jacob Des

Vol. 2

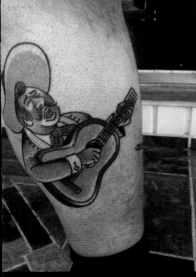

James McKenna

Vol. 3

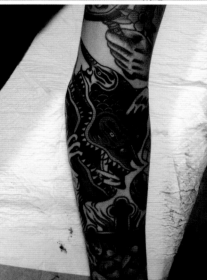

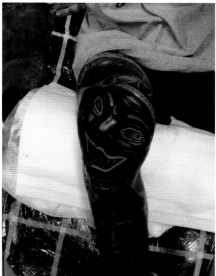

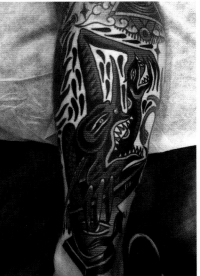

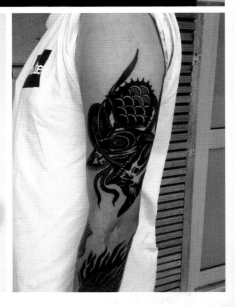

Jasmin Austin

Vol. 2

Jason Donahue

Vol. 5

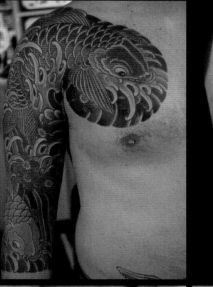

Javier Betancourt

Vol. 5

Jelle Soos

Vol. 4

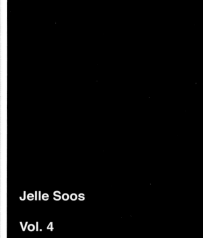

Jenna Slowerblack

Vol. 4

Jim Little

Vol. 5

Joel Melrose

Vol. 5

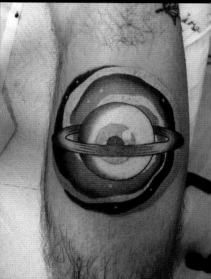

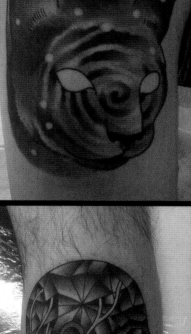

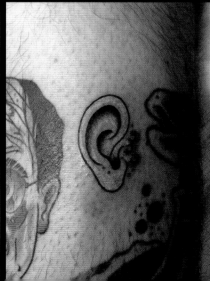
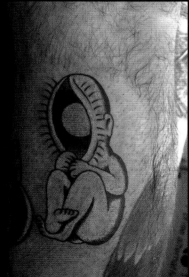
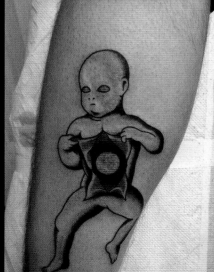

Johann Ingemar

Vol. 4

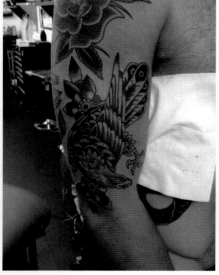

Josh Leahy

Vol. 1

Justin Burnout

Vol. 5

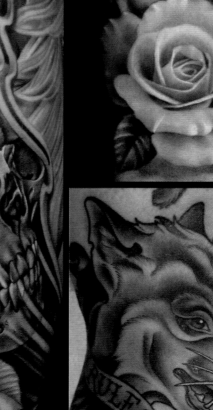

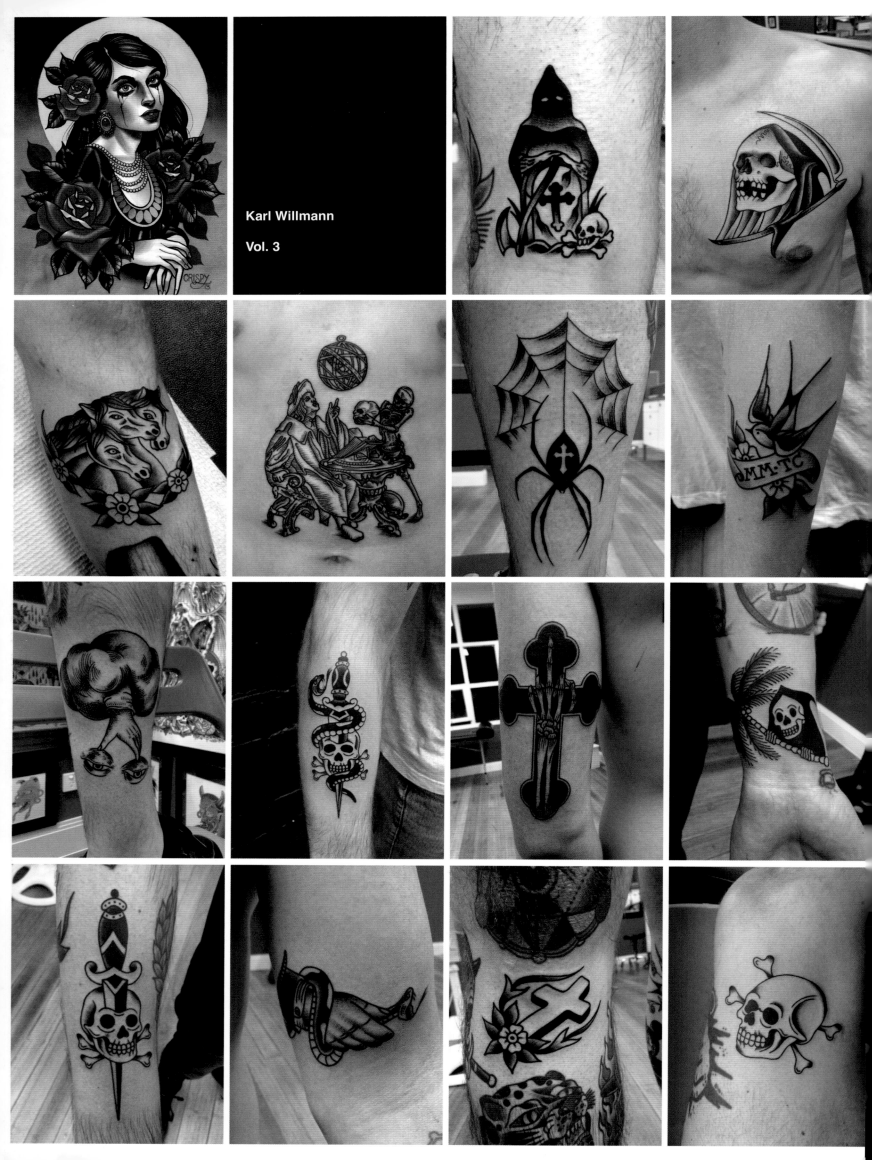

Karl Willmann

Vol. 3

Kid Kross

Vol. 4

Kirk Jones

Vol. 4

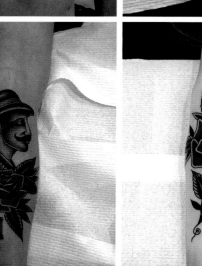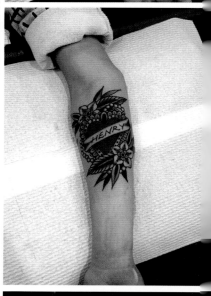

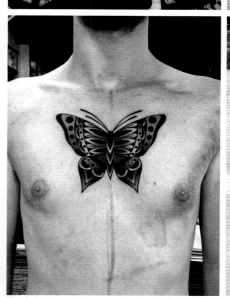

Lauren Winzer

Vol. 4

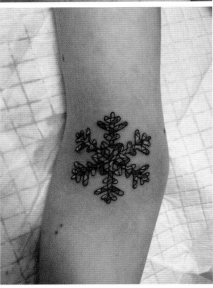

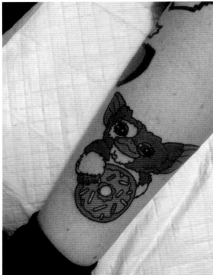

Liam Jenkins

Vol. 3

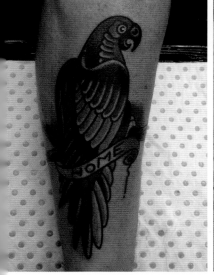

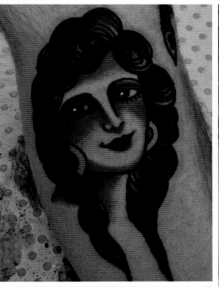

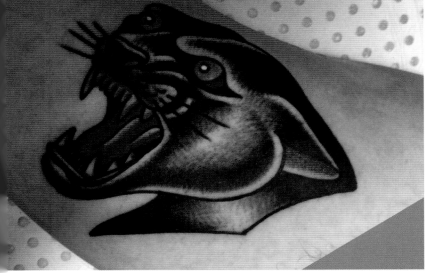

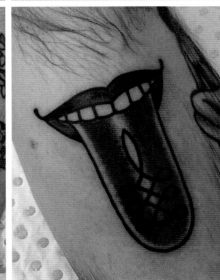

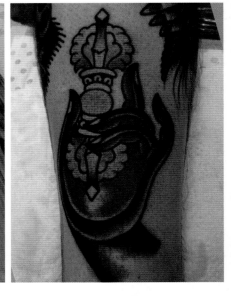

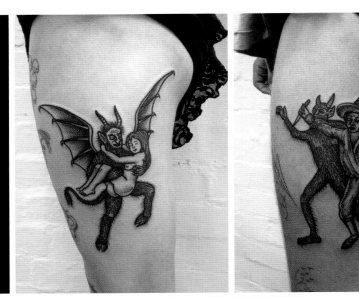

Liam Sparkes

Vol. 4

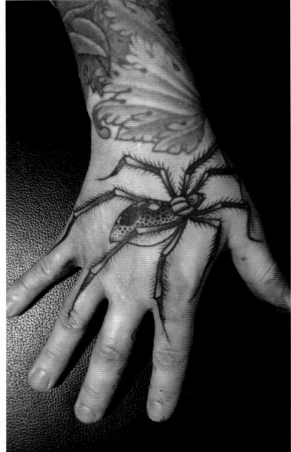

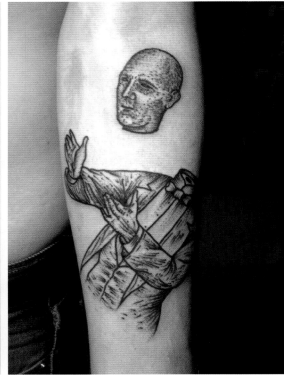

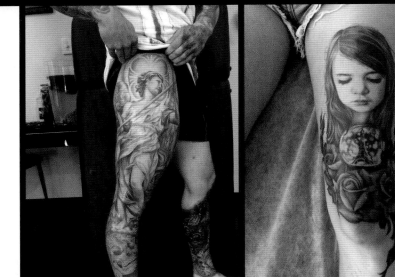

Malika Rose

Vol. 5

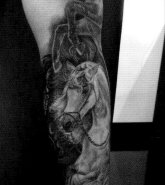

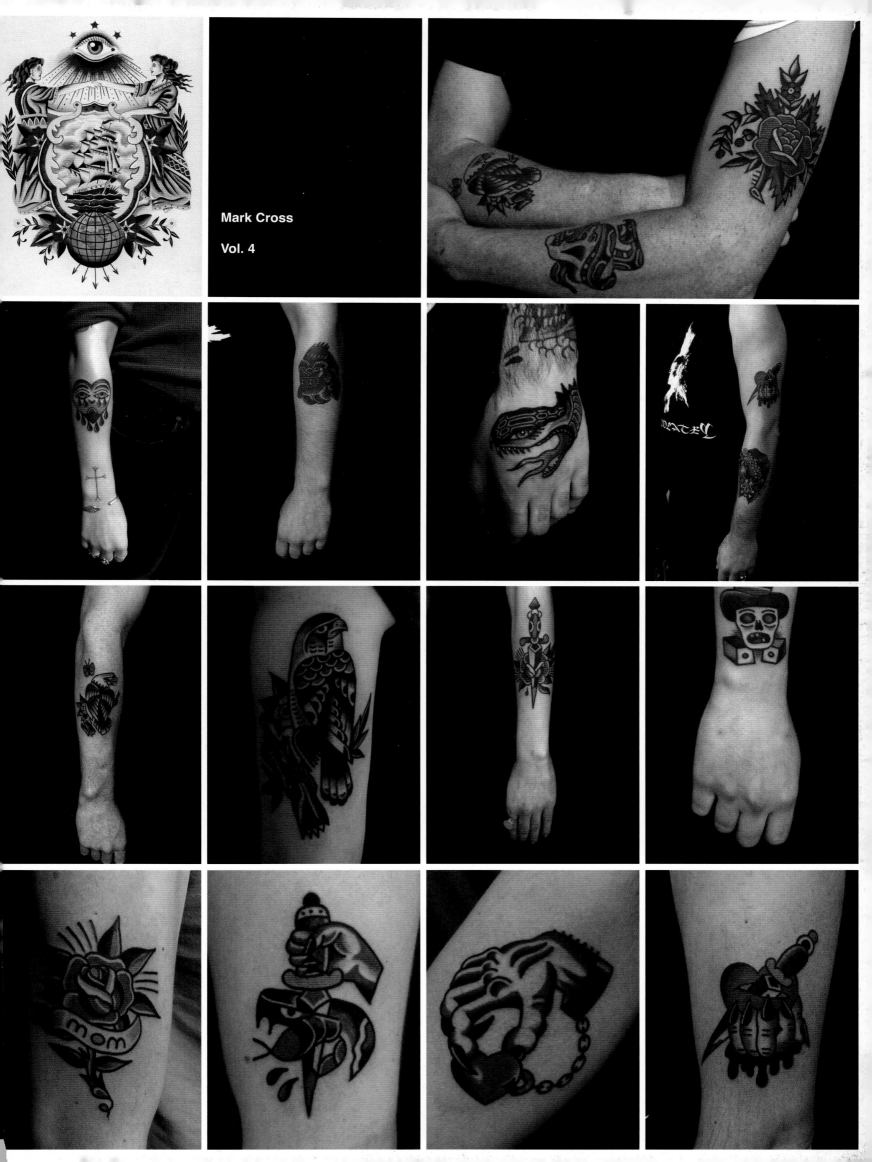

Mark Cross

Vol. 4

Marshall

Vol. 2

Matt Deverson

Vol. 4

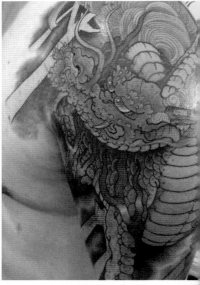

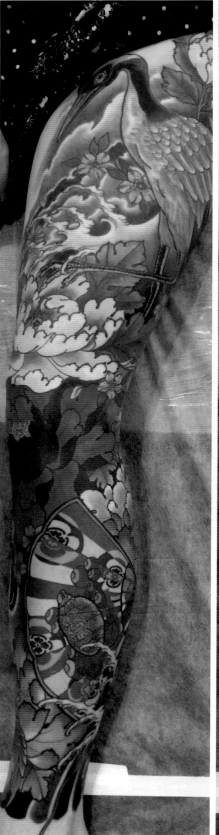

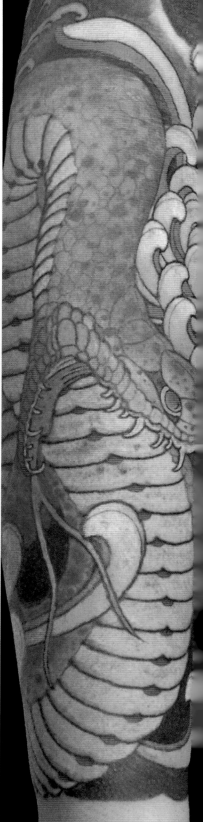

Matt Shamah

Vol. 5

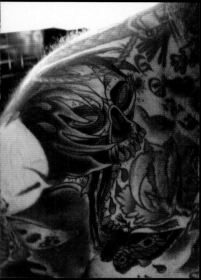

Matt Wisdom

Vol. 2

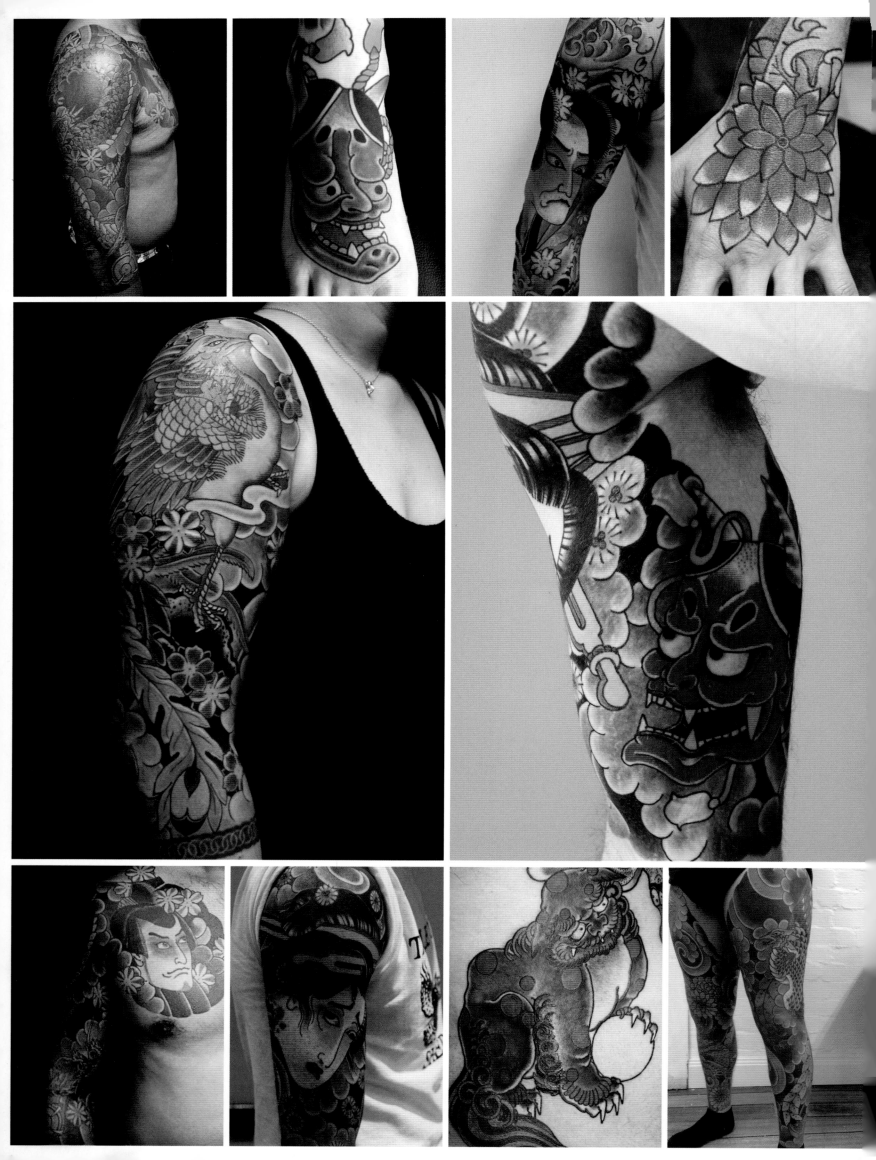

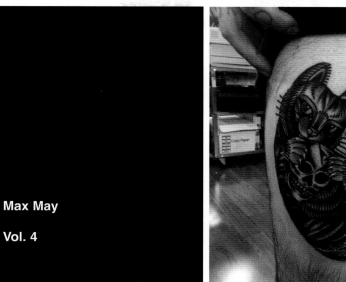

Max May

Vol. 4

Maxime Büchi

Vol. 4

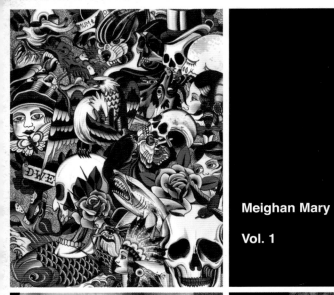

Meighan Mary

Vol. 1

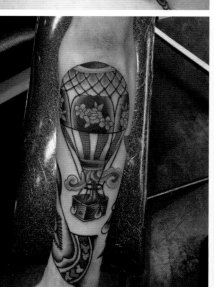

Mick Gore

Vol. 5

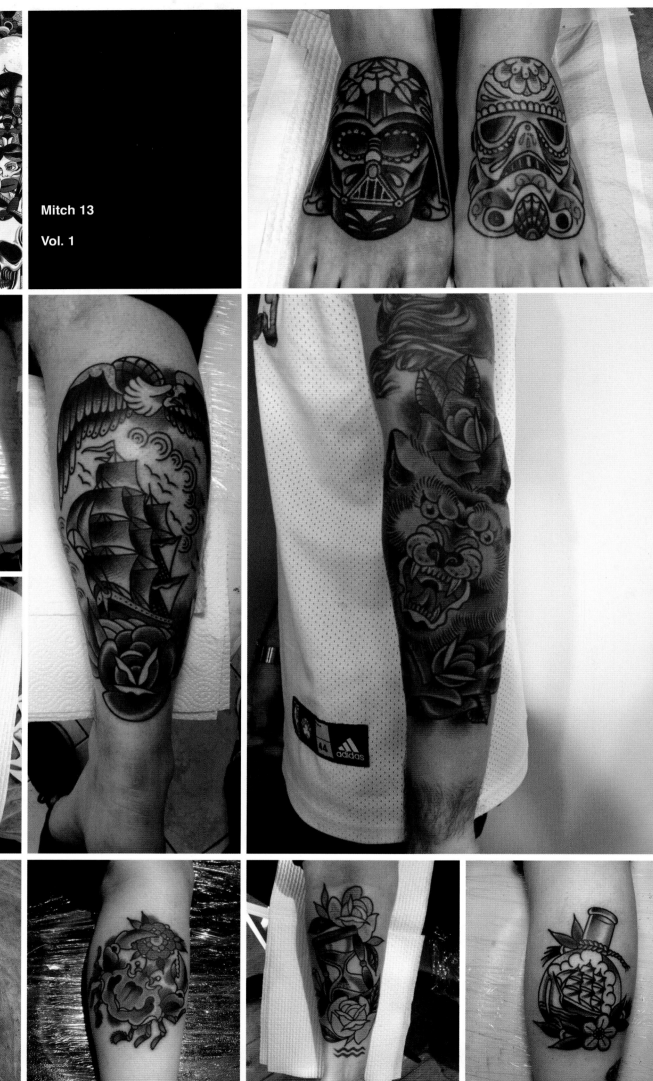

Mitch 13

Vol. 1

Mitch Love

Vol. 5

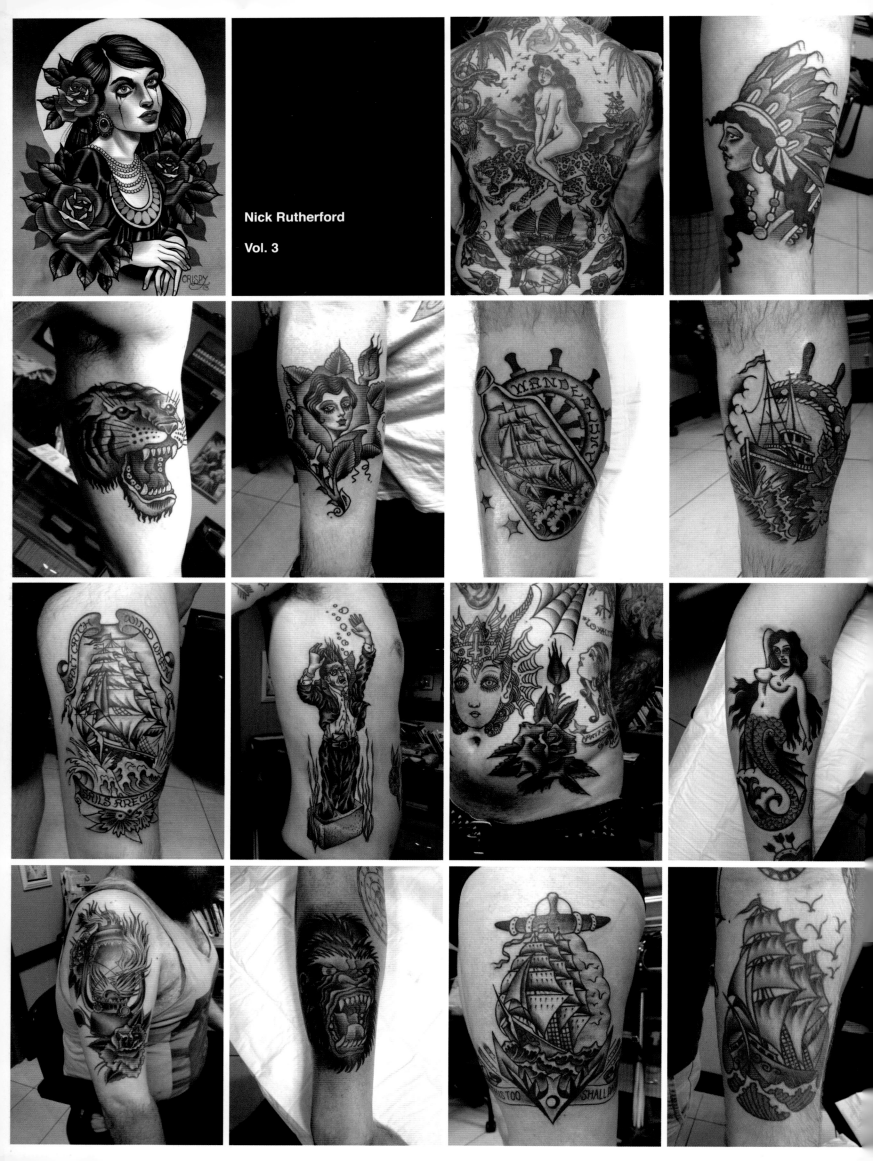

Nick Rutherford

Vol. 3

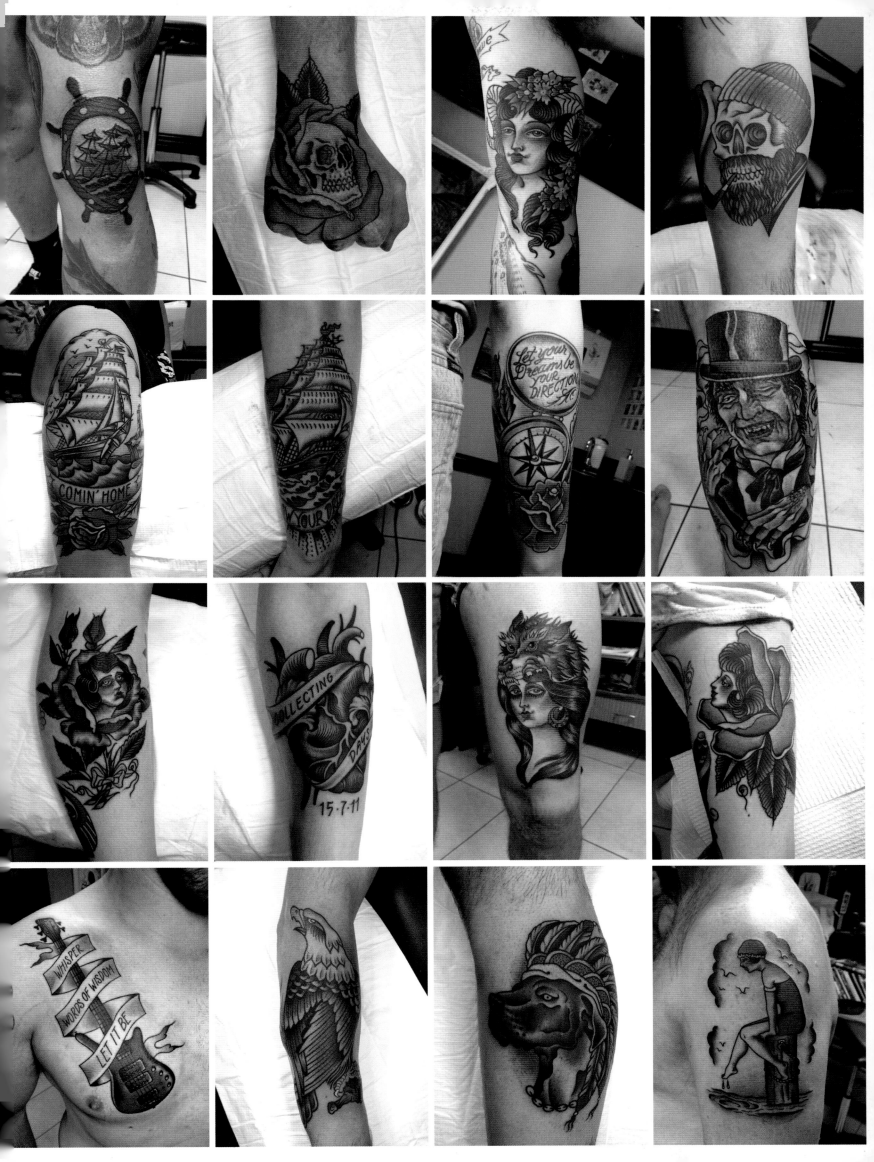

Noah Moore

Vol. 5

Oliver Christenson

Vol. 3

Pari Corbitt

Vol. 3

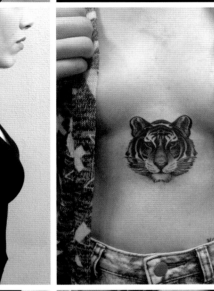

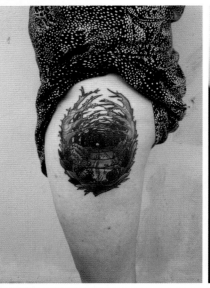

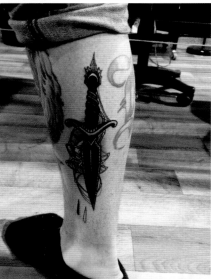

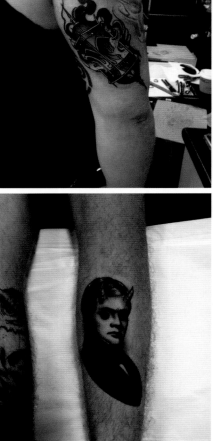
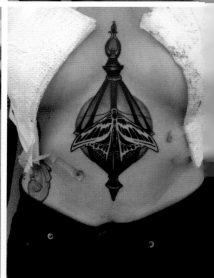
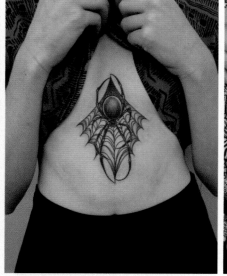

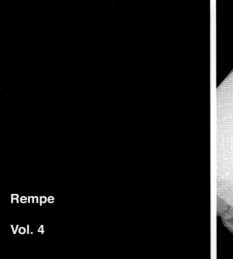

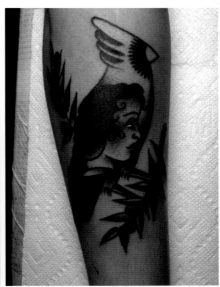

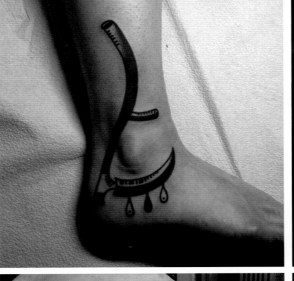

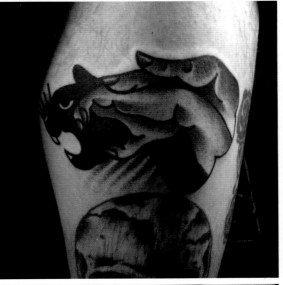

Rich Hardy

Vol. 4

Rose Hardy

Vol. 5

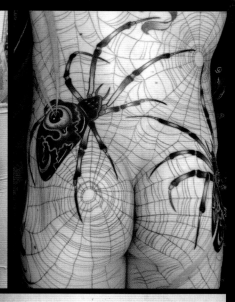

Ryan Shaffer

Vol. 4

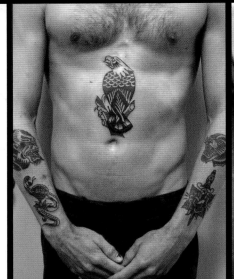

Sal Scutio

Vol. 5

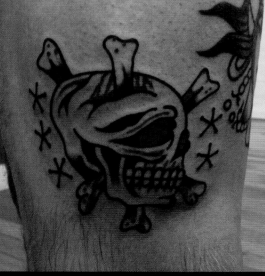

Sam Arrowsmith

Vol. 5

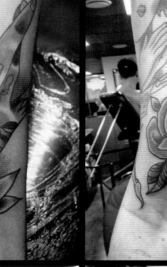

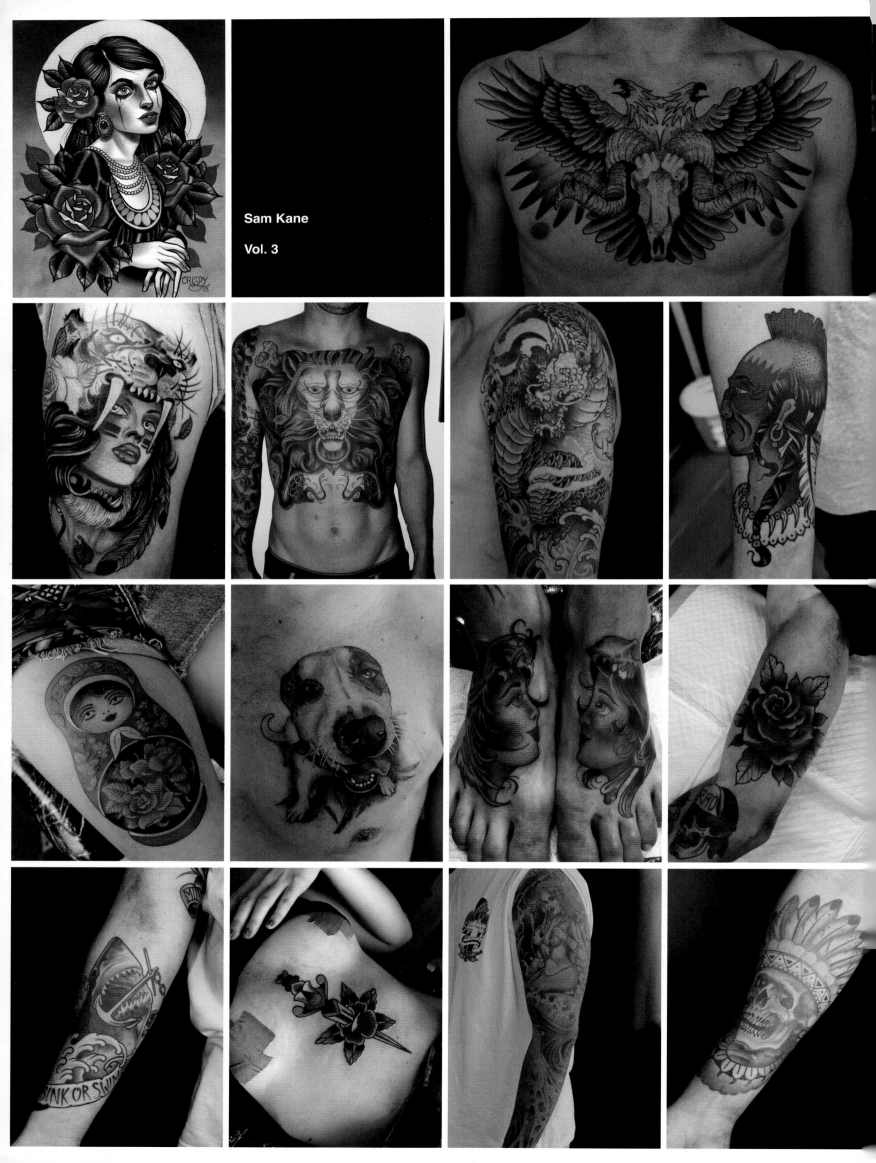

Sam Kane

Vol. 3

Sam Rulz

Vol. 4

Sandi Calistro

Vol. 4

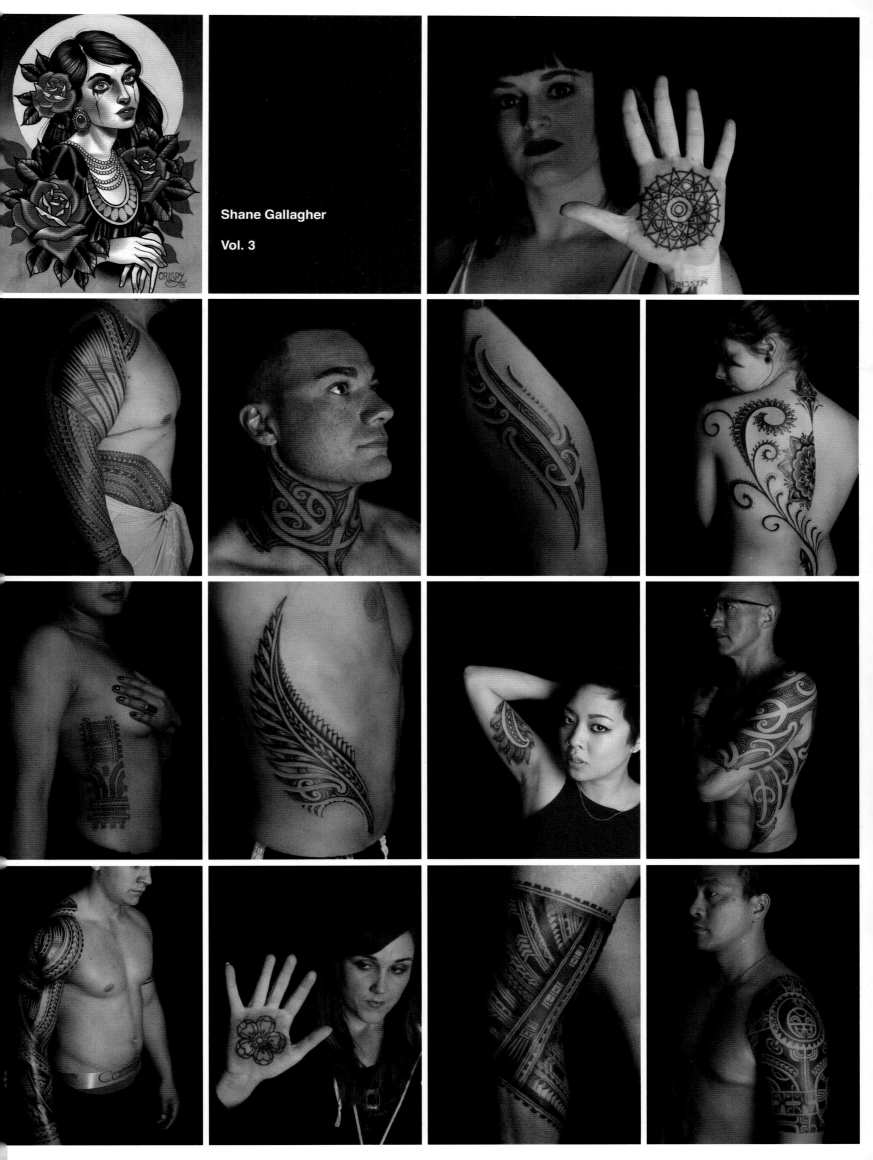

Shane Gallagher

Vol. 3

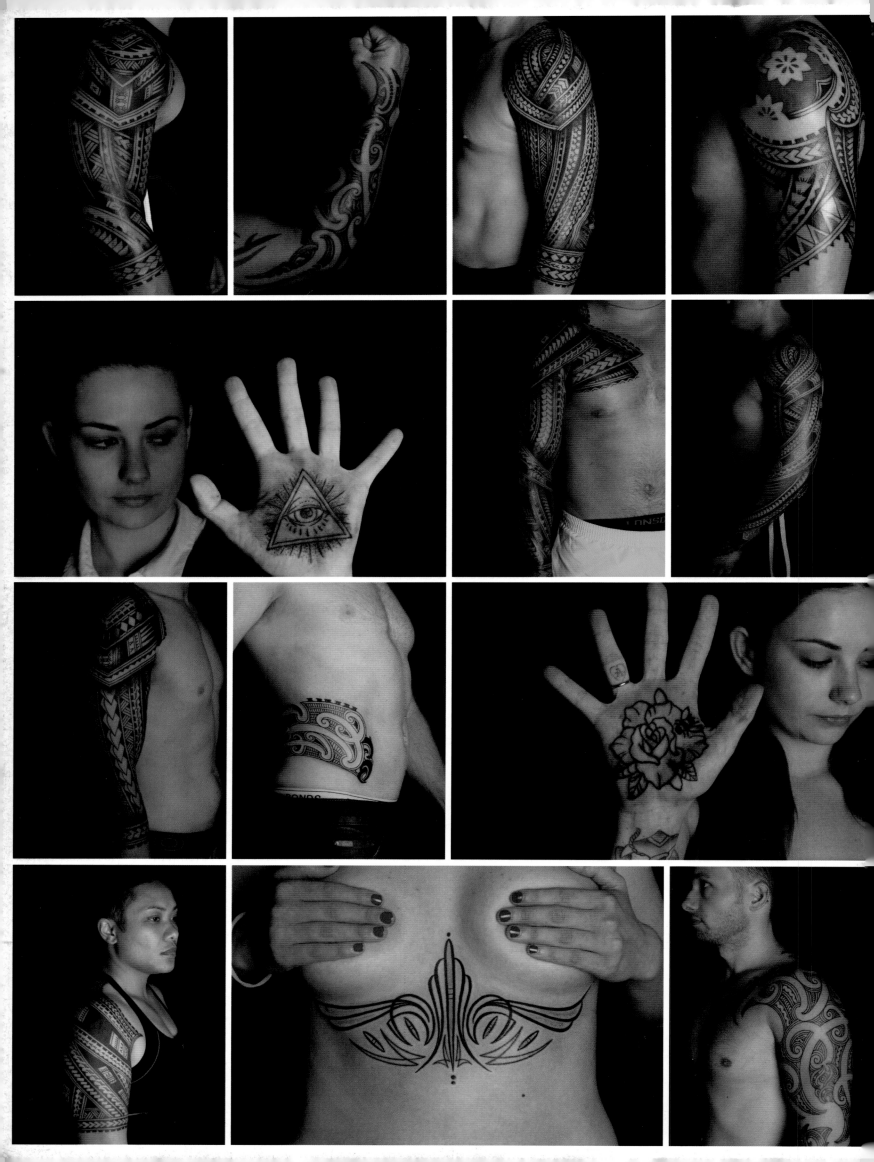

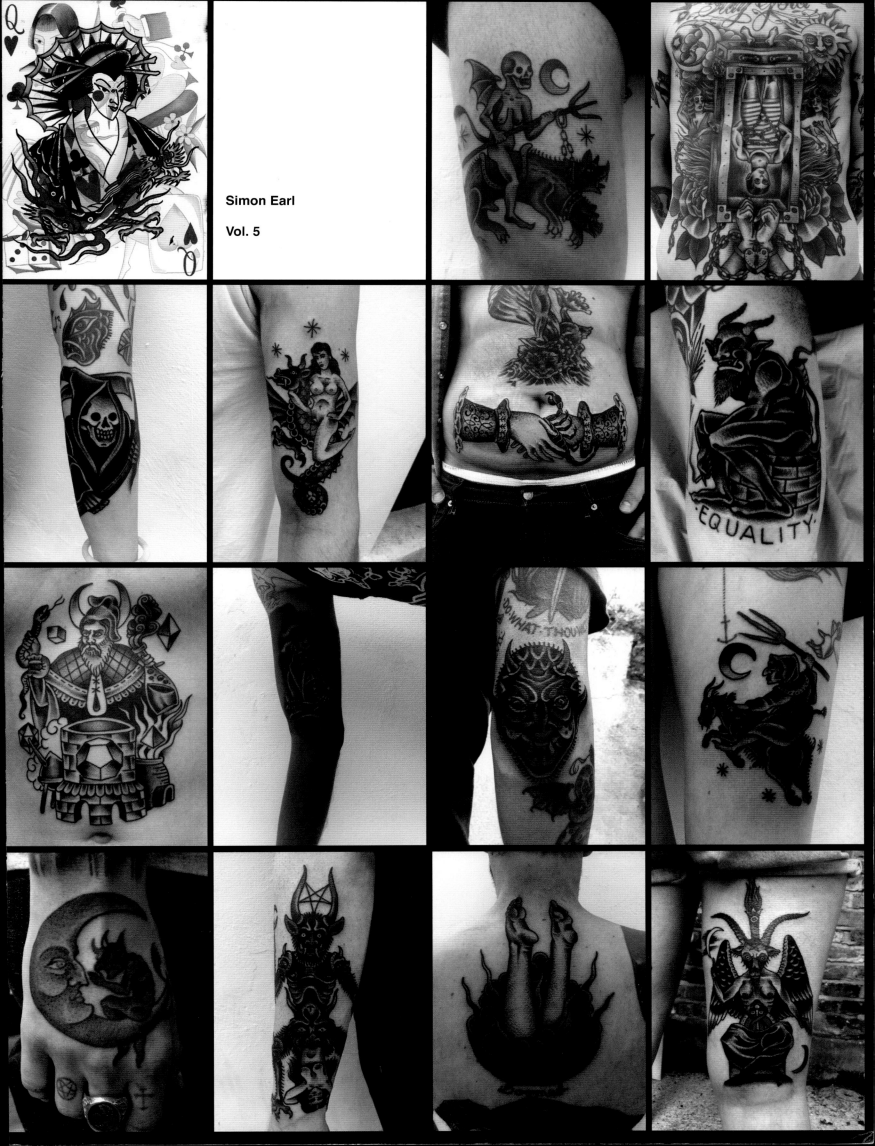

Simon Earl

Vol. 5

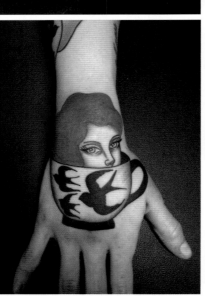

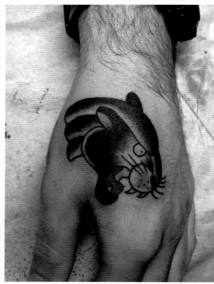

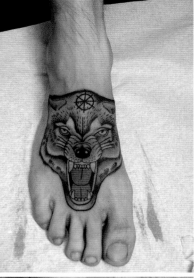

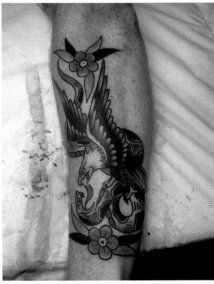

Steve Byrne

Vol. 1

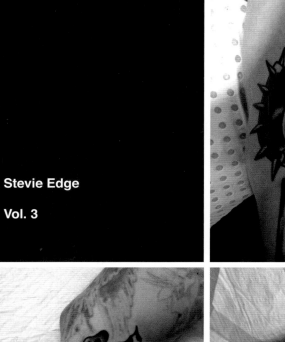

Stevie Edge

Vol. 3

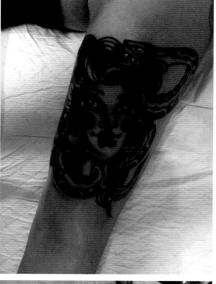

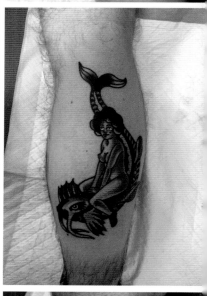

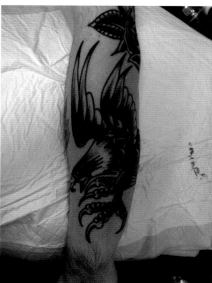

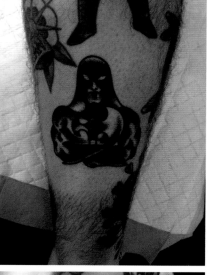

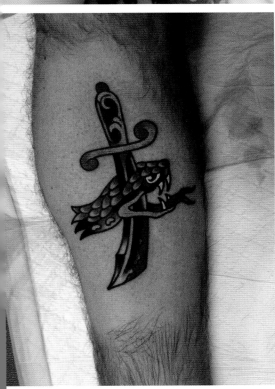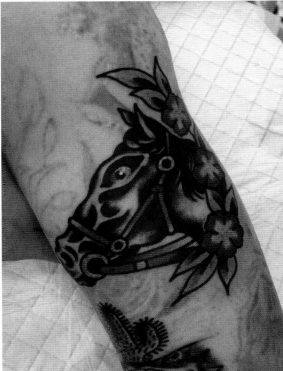

Terry James

Vol. 1

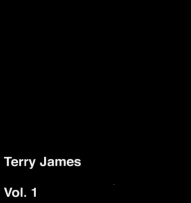

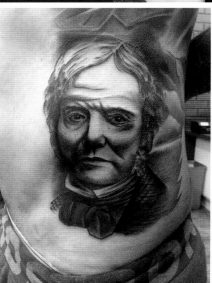

Wan

Vol. 3

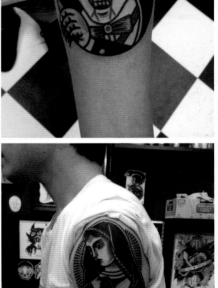

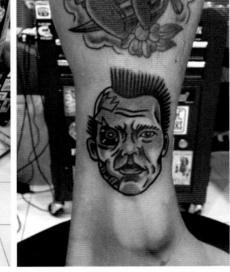

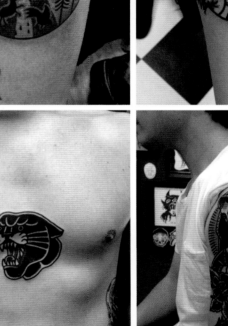

William Yoneyama

Vol. 2

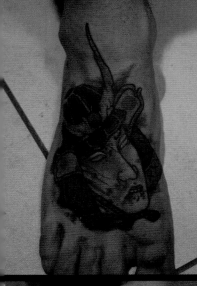

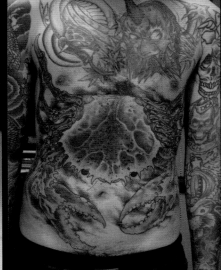

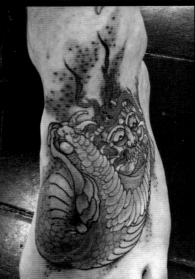

Zoe Dennis

Vol. 2

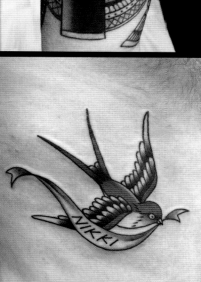

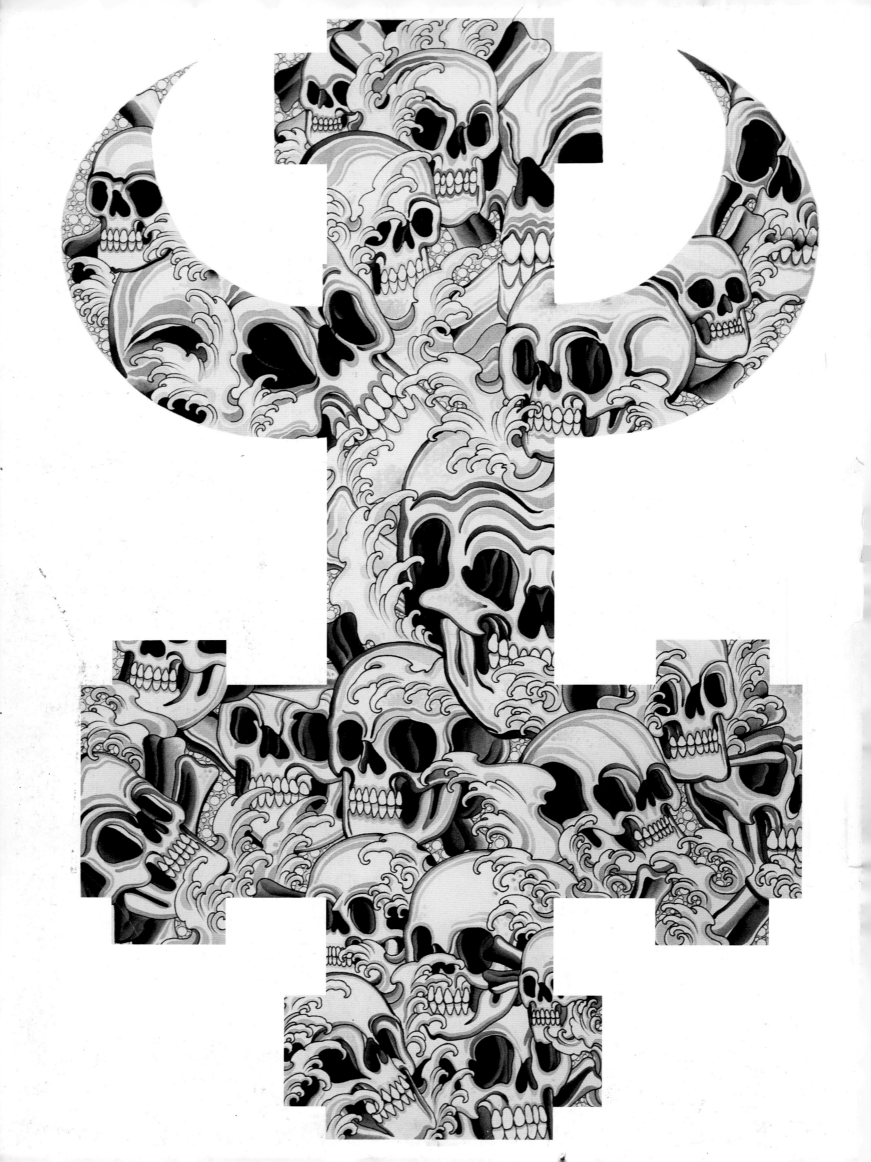